MW00909359

I PRAY GOD'S BEST FOR YOU! Love Necci

My Prayer Is:

Whispers and Wisdoms for the Heart

By

Necci Headen Cooper

Published by
Queen V Publishing
Englewood, OH
QueenVPublishing.com

Published by
Queen V Publishing
Englewood, OH
QueenVPublishing.com

Library of Congress Catalog Number: 2021902492

ISBN-13: 978-0-9962991-5-2

Edited by Valerie J. Lewis Coleman of Pen of the Writer PenOfTheWriter.com

Printed in the United States of America

Dedication

To Jesus Christ,

the One

Who made this journey possible

and to everyone I love.

Table of Contents

Prayer Whisper II

Prayer Whisper III

From the Author's Heart

My prayer is:

You always seek encouragement through
His Word and prayer.
As you turn each page of life,
I hope your heart is stirred
and your soul refreshed.
My desire is for you to experience
a productive, prosperous and beautiful journey
on a deeper, more intimate level.
As you reach for diamonds in the sky,
go beyond the silvery moon
to touch the Son.

I call on You, my God
for You will answer me,
turn Your ear to me
and hear my prayer.
—Psalm 17:6 NIV

Introduction

Prayer is your heart connection to God. Your petition declares you need Him in all situations. Whether you petition the Father on behalf of someone or you're on the receiving end, prayer is essential for every believer. Spoken aloud or echoed in your heart, long or short, your soul gets His attention.

I am a poet who is fascinated by how God masterfully uses words to change the heart. When inspiration meets prayer, they join into a poetic marriage to create life harmony.

I never thought I would pen a book of prayers because it is easier to stick to what I know—poetry—rather than change lanes. Change is sometimes inconvenient and often unexpected; however, I heeded His voice.

At the end of each section, I provided space for you to journal your thoughts, capture your feelings and talk to God. Let's walk together on your journey to self-discovery, prayer and God's love. I encourage you to read the Bible and pray daily to understand and receive the full benefit of His promises. Know that when you experience the ebb and flow of life, He waits to hear from you.

Necci Headen Cooper

Prayer Whisper I

Prayer lifts your soul off life's threshing floor.

Use its power to rise.

The Sun's Light

My prayer is:

Wake up with the sun's light shining
in His brilliance and glory upon your face.
Feel God's presence
bringing comfort and soul-filling warmth
to your heart.

Evolve Your Thoughts

My prayer is:

Allow God's teachings
to evolve your inner thoughts.
When Divine revelation arrives
in your heart,
drastic change will occur.
Let new life transformation begin.

The Morning Star

My prayer is:

As the Morningstar illuminates the darkened skies,
with the Earth passing slowly through its universe,
trust the Lord, obey His command
by loving Him with every beat of your heart.

Call Upon God

My prayer is:

Use contentment of your inner soul
to raise the level of happiness.
Call upon God for unspeakable joy,
find its laughter and peace.
Let your heart experience His jubilee.

Fulfill His Plan

My prayer is:

Prepare your soul to receive
God's natural and spiritual resources
needed to fulfill His plan.
May your heart be filled with plenty
and your barns be made full.

God's Beautiful Nature

My prayer is:

Be influenced by God's beautiful nature.
Allow His Word to come to fruition,
changing your life perspective.
Watch blessings unfold
like He promised to those who dare believe.

Nothing is Impossible

My prayer is:

Never be afraid to ask God
for anything impossible.
Nothing is impossible with Him,
when you let your heart believe that.

Life Adjustments

My prayer is:

Make the necessary life adjustments
when things do not turn out your way,
know that God's thoughts are higher.
His way is not your way,
it is the best way.

Give God First Place

My prayer is:

Focus on your heart. Give God first place.
Decrease so that He can increase.
Never stop praying, forgiving, and loving
because these things are why
life makes sense.

Acquire God's Wisdom

My prayer is:

Never see failure as the end.

See failure as a way to learn.

Acquire God's wisdom.

You will need it to accomplish

Kingdom work,

the next time around.

Hear God's Voice

My prayer is:

Allow silence to be your golden.
Speak less.
Allow your heart to listen more,
then the ability to hear God's voice
becomes more prominent than your own.

Five Smooth Stones

My prayer is:

Carry your slingshot of faith, mercy, obedience,
love, and TRUTH.
Use these five smooth stones
to slay life's giants.

As the River Flows

My prayer is:

As the river flows like rushing waves
through your life,
withstand its current.
Head into the direction
of God's push
bringing your destiny to shore.

Life's Canvas

My prayer is:

Resist the urge to rush matters into

your own hands.

Learn the art of patience.

Life's canvas is more beautiful

when you wait on Him

with the right paintbrush.

Eyes Ready, Heart Steady

My prayer is:

Adjust yourself for a life shift.
The plans you have may differ from God's will
and He will change them
without advance notice.
Keep your eyes ready
and your heart steady.

Sleeping Lion Within

My prayer is:

Awaken the sleeping lion within

for God's purpose to come into your life.

Desire it so deeply

that the tallest mountain

hears you roar.

Life Boundaries

My prayer is:

Establish necessary boundaries
allowing the Lord to enlarge your territory
across nations
and according to His will,
walk out the passion of your heart.

Your Life Song

My prayer is:

Refuse to become
disillusioned by age,
and never let it cripple your soul.
New love, joy, peace, purpose
can be discovered at any stage,
let this melody be your life song.

Leap Tall Buildings

My prayer is:

Never hesitate to step out
on faith, speak the truth in love
or live your life uncompromised.
With God, you can leap tall buildings
in a single bound…jump!

Life Changing Power

My prayer is:

Let God's super connect to
your natural and witness firsthand
the miracle-working, life-changing
power of His Word.

Whispering Your Thoughts

Prayer Whisper II

For greater impact,

think of prayer as not only starting your day,

think of prayer as starting your life.

Your Soul's Music

My prayer is:

Carry a ballad of pure worship
in your heart.
Sing sweet lullabies to the Lord
with instruments of love and thanksgiving
inside your soul's music.

Nourish Your Soul

My prayer is:

Build godly relationships,

and bring something good to share

at the table where your plate is already waiting

to nourish your soul.

God set a placemat just for you.

Time with God

My prayer is:

Devote more "you" time with God.
Whatever your early is, it does not matter
when seeking Him.
He is always waiting
to greet your heart.

Rest in Stillness

My prayer is:

When life vexes your spirit,

rest in stillness.

No need to take this world by storm because

God protects you

from its rain.

Twist of Lime

My prayer is:

Tune your ears to the ones
uplifting your heart.
It is important to hear a kind voice
who refuses to see an empty glass.
They know the greatness God placed in you
and rather see your glass full
with a twist of lime.

Pull in Power

My prayer is:

Rise in confidence, you are adequate.
God made you capable
of pushing every fear aside.
Pull in power, love and a sound mind
because all of these attributes
have been graciously given to you.

Pearls

My prayer is:

Move away from pleasing
those who have little
or NO concern for your heart.
Still love them
as the Lord requires,
but cast your pearls somewhere else.

Handiwork of God

My prayer is:

Begin your day
with tenderness, patience and a heart that loves.
Reveal to others that
you are beautiful handiwork of God
whose soul belongs to Him.

Necci Headen Cooper

Soar Like an Eagle

My prayer is:

Fly like a bluebird swaying
through the gentle wind.
Soar like an eagle
spreading its wings against the clouds
longing to be free.

Reimagine Life

My prayer is:

Reimagine life on a larger scale.

It cost you nothing to dream,

but it may cost, if you do not.

Be excited and listen with an open heart because

its reality comes from God.

Necci Headen Cooper

God's Fresh Air

My prayer is:

Unspin the cocoon entwined around your heart.
Emerge from its wrappings
like the mosaic butterfly
spreading its wings with beauty
into God's fresh air.

Promised Land

My prayer is:

Maneuver your heart through
life's wilderness of fear,
discouragement and rejection,
which is not your destiny.
God has more
promised land for you.

Shared Love

My prayer is:

Find God's presence daily
with a child-like heart.
Nothing is more pleasing and wonderful
than shared love between the Father
and His children.

Flame of God's Love

My prayer is:

Light up your soul
with the flame of God's love.
His power to illuminate
comes through your heart
and darkness gets lost in your shine.

Love Speaks

My prayer is:

Strive to be gentle, sincere and kind.

Turn up the volume!

Love speaks its loudest

when your heart is heard

before you ever say a word.

The Cross Paid

My prayer is:

Invest your life wisely.
If there is no deposit, there is no return.
Understand the high price the Cross paid.
Your worth increases
once you know
the value of your soul.

Live Your Now

My prayer is:

Live your now!
God securely holds your future
with the Word declaring that
tomorrow will take care of itself.
Do NOT miss what needs to be
accomplished today
waiting on the next one.

Higher Ground

My prayer is:

Run away from self-will interference,
irrational emotions, and pride.
God cannot have His way,
if you are in the way—so move
to Higher ground.

Examine Daily

My prayer is:

Examine daily your thought life
to find out where your heart stands
in the Word.
So, when time pushes ahead
the past is left behind you.

Let Him Dwell

My prayer is:

Invite God's glorious presence
to rest over your barren place.
He will graciously accept your invitation
and give your heart greater
capacity to love.
Give Him room to dwell.

Whispering Your Thoughts

Prayer Whisper III

Whether things turn out for better or worse,

turn to God.

Life will change, once your heart changes, so

seek the Kingdom first and all things will be added.

Die on the Cross Love

My prayer is:

When the flesh rises,
kill it with the Word.
Who became flesh
and sacrificed His precious Blood
with His die-on-the-Cross love,
that saved you.

Unexplainable Peace

My prayer is:

When life tests your heart, mind or calm,
pass the exam
by living in graciousness
with unexplainable peace
from the One
Who gives you strength
to endure.

Fresh Waterfall

My prayer is:

For drought to permanently vanish from your life,
and a fresh waterfall of God's promises
and blessings overflow like a river
pouring into your ocean.

Heart of Hearts

My prayer is:

Raise faith and lower doubt
by sincerely believing in
your heart of hearts
the everlasting and unfailing
beautiful love of God.

Pause Your Heart

My prayer is:

Pause your heart.

Whatever untimely situation may appear,

it is temporary.

Treat it as such

and let God

handle His business.

Seed

My prayer is:

If you cannot see the forest,

where there are NO trees

plant something that will grow exceedingly

with the seed

God has given you.

Necci Headen Cooper

See Level

My prayer is:

When rising waters of life
go above ***see*** level,
activate your faith
for evidence not seen.

Grow Taller

My prayer is:

In moments when mistakes are made,

falling short

makes you want to

grow taller.

Inspire Your Pulse

My prayer is:

Be careful of the words you speak.

God hears each one,

the adversary does, too.

The power in words can change the trajectory of your life.

Either they will poison your heart

or inspire your pulse.

Turn Off Its Switch

My prayer is:

Detangle your heart
from the clamor of this noisy world.
Slip quietly into God's gates
and turn off its switch
to find the serenity you desire.

Embrace Your Beautiful

My prayer is:

Embrace your beautiful.
Age does NOT matter.
Age does not determine worthiness,
nor success.
You were designed by God
and that settles it.

Life's Canyon

My prayer is:

For you to always experience God's best.
Live strong, humble, unapologetic, joyful
and with great love
while sojourning over the mountaintop
into life's canyon.

Double Portion of His Love

My prayer is:

Allow God to repair your broken vase.
He will give you everything you need
with clear and pristine water
to console your heart,
and a double portion of His love
for your flowers to grow.

Love Soak

My prayer is:

For God to love soak your heart
like an exhilarating rain,
His welcoming Spirit will pour
like a fountain cleansing the earth
of your soul.

One Heart

My prayer is:

Change your approach to
how you see life
in a fallen world.
God graciously bestowed another day.
Start it
with kindness because spreading love
always starts with one heart.

Anchored in Hope

My prayer is:

Be anchored in hope, steady in faith.
Do NOT let life's crashing waves
push you into a place of despair.
Allow God to navigate your peace
and let the ships fall
where they may.

Grow

My prayer is:

Realize excuses DON'T grow you,

they slow you,

which is NOT God's will for your life.

God's True Essence

My prayer is:

Prune dead things by turning off their life-support.
Refuse to resuscitate anything
that keeps you from living inside
God's true essence.

Get to Know Me

My prayer is:

If someone says to you,
"I knew you when...."
Kindly reply,
"Get to know me now because
God has forever changed my heart."

Draw Closer

My prayer is:

Never allow the enemy's words
to kill you softly.
Revitalize your soul and draw closer to God.
Inhale His Word
to exhale a wonderful life.

Whispering Your Thoughts

Prayer Whisper IV

Prayer starts with God

listening to your heart

and ends with you hearing His.

He Moves

My prayer is:

Watch for little
changes in your life.
It is easy to miss God,
when you ONLY look for big things.
He moves both ways.

Avalanche

My prayer is:

Always love completely
with a motiveless and gracious heart
to open an avalanche
of God's goodness into your life.

Recondition Your Heart

My prayer is:

Recondition your heart

with greater expectation of God's promises.

He meant for you

to enjoy an amazing journey,

today is the beginning of something new.

Get Rooted

My prayer is:

Push back from ALL fruitless things
that break your branches, prevent your bloom,
and pull you away from the Tree of Life.
Get rooted in the Word to stand on solid ground.

God's Favor

My prayer is:

For God's favor to overtake you,
bring natural and spiritual increase,
and extend its reach
to everyone connected
to your heart.

Chosen by God

My prayer is:

Continue to discover who you are in Christ.

Gracefully mature in His ways.

Know that feeling unqualified is NOT a factor,

when you are chosen by God.

Sufficient Grace

My prayer is:

Recognize that any display of meekness is
NOT weakness,
but rather evidence of God's strength
to remind you of the
humility, mercy and love, which
exist in your heart
as proof that
His grace is sufficient.

Immerse Yourself

My prayer is:

Relax your heart in God's awesomeness.
Immerse yourself inside
His wonderful wisdom to gain
spiritual discernment through
soul-filled meditation
of His Word day and night.

Reserve Love

My prayer is:

Settle your heart.
Keep loving those
incapable of loving back.
It does not matter,
when you reserve more than enough of
God's love in your soul
to give to others.

God's Command

My prayer is:

Immediate release of the wealth of the wicked
that is laid up for the just,
and blessings be dispatched into this atmosphere
where Heaven yields
to the command of God.

For You

My prayer is:

Do NOT let the enemy
suppress your dreams,
depress your mind or
oppress your soul.
He is an unsavory foe
who God defeated for you.

Be Complete

My prayer is:

Never allow anyone to short change your heart.

You are wonderfully made

in God's perfect image.

Be complete in knowing that.

Flow

My prayer is:

Never accept mediocrity for your life.
It is not your destiny.
The Earth is the Lord's and the fullness thereof!
Hold on as it rotates
and go with His flow.

Appreciate God's Beauty

My prayer is:

Pause a few moments
each day to delight in appreciation of God's beauty
through the eyes of your heart
and observe all of His wonders.

Validator of Your Heart

My prayer is:

Whatever you accomplish,

do it with

sincerity, humility and love.

God is the true Validator of your heart.

Replenish

My prayer is:

Give generously to others.
It prompts the Lord
to replenish your storehouse,
when you cheerfully give to His.

Victory

My prayer is:

Wave the Blood-stained banner
through life's adversities.
It is your victory flag.

Emerge with More

My prayer is:

Rise from beneath life's ashes
into God's beauty;
uncharred and unscarred.
Emerge with more
confidence, humility, wisdom
and love.

Broken Chain

My prayer is:

Every link of the enemy's chain is broken
and the padlock falls off your heart.
The Lord heard your soul wailing.
Stand up in triumph
and come out of the cave
FREE.

Impart God's Sovereignty

My prayer is:

Depart from anything that negatively
invades your heart-space.
Abandon the strongholds of
fear, fallacies and foreign interpretations.
Impart the sovereignty of God.
Resist the devil and he shall flee.

Whispering Your Thoughts

Prayer Whisper V

A quiet conversation in obedience and
a still heart through prayer
create the perfect conduit
connecting the love between you and God.

Beyond the Mirror

My prayer is:

Look beyond the mirror
to see your inner beauty, which is
invisible to the naked eye.
God does NOT want you
concerned with vain superficialities
because He is NOT.
He is looking at your heart.

Refuse to Shrink

My prayer is:

Spend time studying God.
Your devotion is pivotal for growth.
He will teach you
what the world cannot
and give you an overabundance of
love, peace and joy
to the degree your
heart refuses to shrink.

Calm Down

My prayer is:

Calm your soul.
Avoid overthinking on
issues that produce a troubled heart,
second-guessing and nervousness.
Trust God, breathe
and be anxious for nothing.

Not Your Fight

My prayer is:

Realize that NOT everything is yours to fight.

Give it to God.

He is ready, willing and able

to settle ALL matters

concerning your soul.

ALL your battles belong to Him.

Rise Strong

My prayer is:

Keep your heart fixed on God.
Command your day under His authority.
Rise strong in faithfulness, obedience and
righteousness,
calling things that are not
as though they are.

Remove

My prayer is:

For God to remove ALL uncertainty

that causes life to stand still

and you to NOT be still.

Loose Your Dreams

My prayer is:

Move your heart forward.
Loose your dreams into Heaven
and loose them on Earth.
Nothing will ever happen,
if you hide them away
from the One Who makes them true.

Don't Spoil the Vine

My prayer is:

Cease giving into fleshly compromises
that cause you to act contrary
to the Word.
These little foxes
spoil the vine.

Mercy and Love

My prayer is:

When others act ugly,
you act beautiful
by showing them an image of what
God's mercy and love really looks like.

Shooting Star

My prayer is:

If you happen to see a star
shooting through the midnight sky,
reach for it.

Landscape of Your Heart

My prayer is:

Always receive the promises
of God's abundance,
and the landscape of your heart
be made beautiful.

Sweet Words

My prayer is:

For God to reverse every evil,
hurtful and untrue word spoken
that fell into your heart
and for your words to be sweet also.

Healing Virtue

My prayer is:

Absorb the power of God's healing virtue
into your mind, heart and soul.
Touch the hem of His garment
and be made whole.
Your life has been restored.

Touch Him

My prayer is:

Use your heart's voice

to touch Him.

When words cannot be spoken,

and you are unable to move,

even in stillness,

the tears flowing from your soul are

heard by God.

Explode into Greatness

My prayer is:

Whatever you choose to do,
do it with excellence, excitement and expectation
without further explanation.
Explode into the greatness
God perfectly designed for you.

Search for Truth

My prayer is:

Search God for truth, correction and destiny.

Discard the ways of conceit, disobedience, and rebellion.

Instead find clarity from Heaven

letting Divine insight

be your sight.

God's Echo

My prayer is:

Pay close attention to untamed emotions.
Hold back your consent to unkind words
that bring sadness, anger, fear and discouragement.
Listen for God's echo
to lift your soul.

Be Content

My prayer is:

Be content waiting for change of seasons.

Forgo getting ahead of its timing.

Stay on course.

Everything has already been made perfect

by the hand of God.

Launch

My prayer is:

Be mindful of where you take your heart.
What you say
will always find a place to land.
Use the power of the affirming Word of God
to launch your journey.

Crystal Stars

My prayer is:

As you observe crystal stars
wandering across the onyx night,
rediscover God's promises.
Then fall into the sweetest sleep
with Love whispering
upon your heart.

Whispering Your Thoughts

Prayer of Love

Heavenly Father,
I embrace who I am
and refuse to see beauty through the world's lens.
You alone are the Creator,
and I love You, dearly.
With expectation in my heart,
I will follow righteousness' path
in obedience to Your Word.
Your glory forever reigns!
I pray that wisdom, favor, peace, joy, mercy and
love operate in my life at full throttle
without ANY malfunction.
On my journey, I pray that Your Spirit
rests upon me always.
Your presence is welcome
wherever my feet tread.
I declare prosperity to flow
like a never-ending river.
Abba, I pray for protection
from the enemy's snares
as You render
him ineffective over me.
I walk in victory every day.
Salvation is in my house forever.
Amen.

Then you will call upon Me and go and pray to Me,
and I will listen to you.
—Jeremiah 29:12

Let love be without hypocrisy.
Abhor what is evil. Cling to what is good.
Be kindly affectionate to one another with brotherly love,
in honor giving preference to one another
not lagging in diligence, fervent in spirit,
serving the Lord;
rejoicing in hope, patient in tribulation,
continuing steadfast in prayer.
—Romans 12:9-12

About the Author

While many place hope in material things, Necci Headen Cooper masters trusting and hoping in the Father. Her innate passion for prayer, coupled with the desire to empower and encourage others, illuminates, radiates and permeates. Whether released onto the pages of a book or spoken to audiences of thousands, she understands that prayer is essential to every believer. Using prayers, praise and prose, she strives to craft a body of work that inspires you to pursue your God-given purpose.

In her debut book, *My Heart's the Pen of a Ready Writer*, Necci penned words of gentleness and power reflective of God's heart. In her sophomore project, *My Prayer Is: Whispers and Wisdoms for the Heart*, she created epistles of thought-provoking, life-changing prayers. Her creative ingenuity has been commissioned to craft one-of-a-kind works for politicians, pastors and personal inspiration.

For interviews, speaking engagements, and bulk purchases, contact Necci at NecciHeadenCooper.com or necciheadencooper@gmail.com.

About Queen V Publishing

The Doorway to YOUR Destiny!

Go thou and publish abroad the kingdom of God.

—Luke 9:60 ESV

Committed to transforming manuscripts into polished works of art, **Queen V Publishing** is a company of standard and integrity. We offer an alternative that allows the message in YOU to do what it was sent to do for OTHERS.

QueenVPublishing.com

Serving professional speakers and experts to magnify and monetize their message by publishing quality books